Investigating
Fossils

Miriam Coleman

PowerKiDS press.

New York

Published in 2016 by The Rosen Publishing Group, Inc.
29 East 21st Street, New York, NY 10010

First Edition

Editor: Sarah Machajewski
Book Design: Katelyn Heinle

Photo Credits: Cover Witold Skrypczak/Lonely Planet Images/Getty Images; pp. 4, 5 RAYMOND ROIG/AFP/Getty Images; p. 6 Dr Paul A Zahl/Photo Researchers/Getty Images; p. 7 Smit/Shutterstock.com; p. 8 (true form fossil) Marcio Jose Bastos Silva/Shutterstock.com; p. 8 (mold fossil) Tom Grundy/Shutterstock.com; p. 9 (cast fossil) Sombra/Shutterstock.com; p. 9 (trace fossil) Julio Embun/Shutterstock.com; p. 10 Bill Florence/Shutterstock.com; p. 11 Stephen J Krasemann/All Canada Photos/Getty Images; p. 12 Imfoto/Shutterstock.com; p. 13 Homebrew Films Company/Gallo Images/Getty Images; p. 15 Harold Brodrick/Science Source/Photo Researchers/Getty Images; p. 17 (rock texture) Geoff Hardy/Shutterstock.com; p. 18 Ariadne Van Zandbergen/Lonely Planet Images/Getty Images; p. 19 TOM MCHUGH/Photo Researchers/Getty Images; p. 21 Sumikophoto/Shutterstock.com; p. 22 Anthony Bradshaw/Photodisc/Getty Images.

Library of Congress Cataloging-in-Publication Data

Coleman, Miriam, author.
 Investigating fossils / Miriam Coleman.
     pages cm. — (Earth science detectives)
 Includes index.
 ISBN 978-1-4777-5943-1 (pbk.)
 ISBN 978-1-4777-5944-8 (6 pack)
 ISBN 978-1-4777-5942-4 (library binding)
 1. Fossils—Juvenile literature. 2. Paleontology—Juvenile literature. 3. Formations (Geology)—Juvenile literature. I. Title.
 QE714.5.C655 2015
 560—dc23
                                      2014028876

Manufactured in the United States of America

CPSIA Compliance Information: Batch #WS15PK: For Further Information contact Rosen Publishing, New York, New York at 1-800-237-9932

CONTENTS

FINDING FOSSIL CLUES

Earth is filled with clues about its past. Like burglars leaving footprints, plants and animals that lived long ago left behind traces, called fossils. The scientists who study these fossils are called paleontologists.

Paleontologists are like detectives. They search fossils for clues about what kinds of creatures lived in an area and what kinds of plants once grew there. They can use these clues to learn more about what life was like before people were here and when and why some creatures disappeared. They can also use the clues to learn how Earth has changed over time.

A paleontologist uses special tools to uncover remains from the past.

Paleontologists must work slowly and carefully when searching for fossils.
They don't want the fossils to break or crumble.

WHAT IS A FOSSIL?

Fossils are the hardened remains of plants and animals that lived at least 10,000 years ago. Fossils are **evidence** of prehistoric life, which refers to things that lived before humans began keeping records.

Fossils can be bones and shells of animals, leaves and seeds of plants, or even footprints and tracks that have lasted through the years. Most fossils come from the hard parts of animals and plants, since these are more likely to survive over time than soft body parts or tracks. Sometimes, however, fossils can be entire animals that became stuck or trapped in tar or **resin**.

This ancient bug was trapped in resin millions of years ago.

From afar, this may have looked like just a plain old rock,
but it actually holds evidence of a creature that lived long ago.

KINDS OF FOSSILS

There are four main kinds of fossils. They all hold important clues about ancient Earth.

True form fossils are the actual creatures or their body parts. Mold fossils are **impressions** of plants and animals that were buried in mud, clay, or other matter that turned into stone. These fossils form open spaces that could be filled up with something. If they are, they become cast fossils.

CLUE ME IN

Coprolites are pieces of fossilized animal waste. Sometimes, coprolites contain the fossils of other animals!

true form fossil

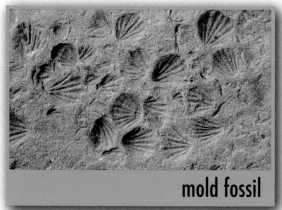
mold fossil

Cast fossils are made when **minerals** fill mold fossils and then harden, creating forms that take the shape of whatever made the impressions. Finally, trace fossils are footprints, tracks, tunnels, or other evidence of activity that animals leave behind.

trace fossil

cast fossil

The fact that these fossils form in different ways and look different teaches us a lot about how conditions on Earth changed over the years.

HOW DO FOSSILS FORM?

Some parts of an animal, such as bones, shells, and teeth, are strong enough to last throughout time. They become fossils when minerals such as quartz, pyrite, or silica take the place of original parts of an **organism**, making it harder and stronger. Petrified wood is an example of this.

Trace fossils form when soft mud containing animal tracks hardens and becomes covered in rock. Sometimes an entire animal—such as a woolly mammoth—is frozen solid after being buried in soil. This very rare kind of fossil contains the animal's **preserved** skin, **muscles**, and hair.

CLUE ME IN

Petrified wood is ancient trees or logs whose plant matter was broken down and filled with minerals. This happens naturally, without any human help!

It's hard to imagine woolly mammoths ever walked the earth, but fossils don't lie. This fossil proves woolly mammoths once existed, which also tells us Earth once had conditions that supported this kind of animal.

THAT'S SEDIMENTARY!

There have been countless plants and animals on Earth, but not all have left behind fossils. In order for an organism to become a fossil, it must be buried before other animals eat it or weather destroys it.

The mud and sand that cover an organism's remains are called sediments. The sediments pile up in **layers** around and on top of the remains. The **pressure** of the growing layers turns the sediment into a hard rock called sedimentary rock. This rock covering can protect and preserve a fossil for many millions of years.

CLUE ME IN
Shale and limestone are two types of sedimentary rock in which fossils are often found.

How could these ancient starfish be found in rocks and not in the sea?
These fossils are a clue that this part of Earth was once covered by water.

FOSSIL HOTSPOTS

Fossils have been found nearly everywhere on Earth, but in some places more than others. The Morrison Formation in the United States is a huge area of rock that was once covered by rivers. Dinosaurs such as *Diplodocus*, *Apatosaurus*, and *Stegosaurus* were buried and preserved here. You can view these fossils at Dinosaur National Monument.

China's Liaoning Province holds thousands of fossils. When the animals there died, they often washed into streams and were buried in ash from volcanoes. The fossils are preserved so well that you can still see skin, feathers, and food inside the animals' stomachs!

CLUE ME IN

The Burgess Shale in the Canadian Rockies is an ancient seabed. It holds very rare fossils of many kinds of soft-bodied animals from 505 million years ago.

Dinosaurs lived during a time in history called the Mesozoic Era.
Scientists use well-preserved dinosaur fossils to learn what Earth was like during this ancient age.

UPLIFT AND EXPOSURE

Most fossils will never be found because they're contained in rocks deep in the ground. However, forces inside Earth cause its surface to change, and rocks that were once underground are brought to the surface. This process is called uplift.

As rock layers are worn away by wind, water, and ice, the fossils become **exposed**. Paleontologists must find them quickly. Once the rock layers that surrounded the fossils are gone, there's nothing left to keep weather and other natural forces from breaking down the fossils. If nobody finds the fossils, they'll be lost for good.

Uplift and exposure are part of the rock cycle. The rock cycle is the process of forming and breaking down rocks. This process doesn't just give us fossils. It also gives Earth the minerals living things need to survive, building matter for people to use, and natural beauty for us to enjoy.

THE ROCK CYCLE

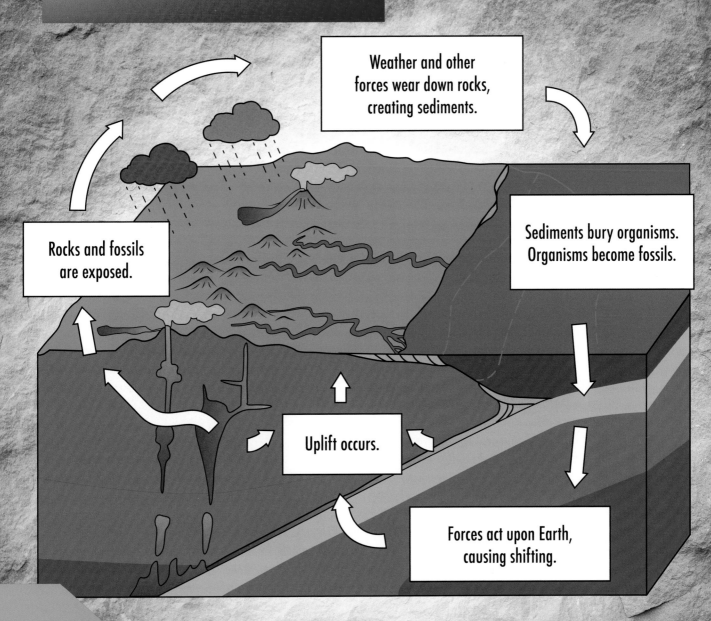

Weather and other forces wear down rocks, creating sediments.

Rocks and fossils are exposed.

Sediments bury organisms. Organisms become fossils.

Uplift occurs.

Forces act upon Earth, causing shifting.

Fossil discoveries have led to major changes in the way we understand Earth's history. In 1676, someone discovered a huge bone thought to be from a giant man. Eventually, scientists decided remains such as this actually belonged to creatures so different they needed their own name—dinosaurs.

CLUE ME IN

The fossils of Lucy's leg bones tell us she walked on two legs. Scientists learned this by looking at how the bones come together and how they move.

When paleontologists put Lucy's bones together, they saw the bones looked much like those of a modern human.

In 1861, a fossil of the oldest winged bird, *Archaeopteryx*, was found in Germany. The *Archaeopteryx*'s feathers suggested it may have been the link between birds and feathered dinosaurs. In 1974, remains of a 3.2 million-year-old human **ancestor** were found in Ethiopia. Nicknamed "Lucy," the fossil gave important information about how human beings developed.

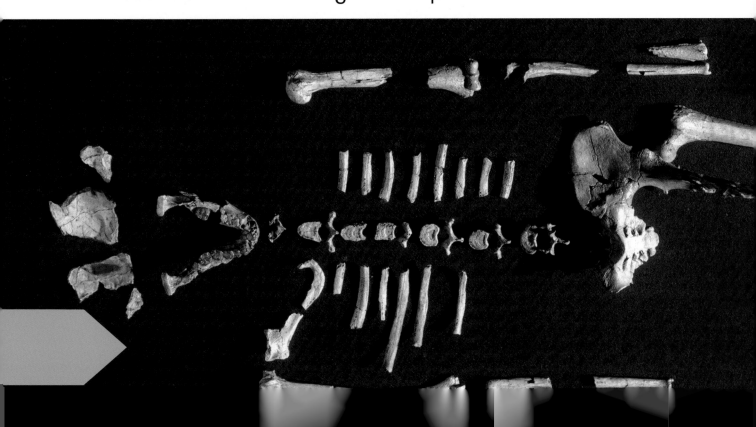

DATING THE FOSSIL

Paleontologists use different methods to learn how old fossils are. One way is by looking at the layers of sedimentary rock. The bottom layers of rock were deposited first, so fossils found there are the oldest. Fossils in the higher layers are more recent. If a different type of rock cuts through those layers, paleontologists know that Earth's forces pushed it through after the other layers formed. That makes the different rock younger than the rest of the layers.

Scientists can get a better idea of how old rocks and fossils are by measuring the amount of carbon, a kind of matter, in them. This is called carbon dating.

What's hidden inside these colorful rock layers? They may contain clues about life in the past.

PRESERVING EARTH'S PAST

Only a small number of creatures leave behind fossils, but they can help us sort out many mysteries about Earth's past. They can show us what animals and plants looked like, when they lived, and when they died out.

Fossils can also show how Earth has changed. Fossilized ferns found in cold places are clues that it was once much warmer there. The same fossils found oceans apart suggest that the continents were once closer together. What could fossils forming now tell the future about today's Earth?

GLOSSARY

ancestor: An animal that lived before others in its family tree.

evidence: Facts, signs, or information that proves something to be true.

expose: To leave something uncovered or unprotected.

impression: A mark left as a result of applying pressure on something.

layer: One thickness lying over or under another.

mineral: Nonliving matter found in nature.

muscle: A collection of tissues that helps an animal or person move parts of their body.

organism: A plant, animal, or other life-form.

preserve: To keep something in its original state.

pressure: The force that acts against an object.

resin: A sticky liquid that some trees make to cover holes in their bark.

INDEX

WEBSITES

Due to the changing nature of Internet links, PowerKids Press has developed an online list of websites related to the subject of this book. This site is updated regularly. Please use this link to access the list: www.powerkidslinks.com/det/foss